MW01221947

Salt Physic

Jacqueline Larson

PEDLAR PRESS | Toronto

ACKNOWLEDGEMENTS
The publisher wishes to thank the Canada Council
for the Arts and the Ontario Arts Council for their
generous support of our publishing program.

LIBRARY AND ARCHIVES CANADA
CATALOGUING IN PUBLICATION

Larson, Jacqueline
    Salt physic / Jacqueline Larson.

Poems.
ISBN 978-1-897141-24-3

    I. Title.

PS8623.A7735S24 2008   C811'.6   C2008-906565-4

DESIGN Zab Design & Typography, Toronto

TYPEFACES Scotch Modern (body) *with* Figgins
(headings) from the Scotch Modern Suite by
Nick Shinn

COVER includes image *Summer Rain* by Wendy Cain

Printed in Canada

THE CANADA COUNCIL | LE CONSEIL DES ARTS
FOR THE ARTS | DU CANADA
SINCE 1957 | DEPUIS 1957

ONTARIO ARTS COUNCIL
CONSEIL DES ARTS DE L'ONTARIO

in memory of my grandmothers

Sylvia Larson (Swasey) 1909-1995

Rosella Stuart (Williams) 1919-1997

Contents

11   Dreams Then

12   Found: In a Slush Pile

16   Self Portrait in Five Weddings

21   Three Songs: Participation Mystique

24   The Blue Dress

26   Rhubarb

31   Salt Lick

36   Not Enough Has Been Said

38   Erratic

42   Salt Physic

48   That Catholic Country

50   On Hiding

53   Cleavage: An Education

56   Negatives

57   Blood Line

60   Through the Word West

70   Brief Biography of One

74   *Notes*

76   *Acknowledgements*

Salt Physic

Dreams Then

If I jump from the train into the river
if we practise our escape
if we wade into the water
if there are green islands
and a woman with a boat
if there are money problems and Flemish paintings
if we can hide our tracks—
there was a cave, a crime scene, a hungry
child blue with cold—
if various points on my forehead burst out bleeding
if Jane Urquhart finds us boring
if no one respects black bears anymore
and passersby won't get involved
if I've become a ghost in an underground
labyrinth or a street lined with roses
if I stumble before I walk barefoot on the ground
in an unnamed city
if I have to travel in order to fly
I don't know how else to explain the
writer's hands on my chest
saying let the light out.

Found: In a Slush Pile

1

The book is not in chapters. It has sixty-eight figures.
It proves that Helena Blavatsky was aware of the real
origin of the Tarot, why the Tower appears
under attack from a giant feather, and the hidden
patterns in ordinary life. It discusses
Mesopotamian artifacts, the history of art and language studies,
Rumi's nighttime rendezvous with extraterrestrials,
King Solomon and brain hemisphere specialization,
the sensation of new insights.

I have included references to popular culture, the Tarot's Lovers,
the Tree of Life, and misunderstood Arabic words.
I discuss Gurdjieff's account of the origin of the moon,
Noah's ark, divine archetypes, and why ravens are
no good for some things.
There are no competing books.

2

Sir/madam!

In the interests of moral

truth, a table of contents,

a step forward in ethical

thought, a new word in science

and philosophy, a synthesis of

ethics and psychology. It is psychological

dialectics and dialectic psychology,

moral psychoanalysis and an evolutionary

theory. With a classical basis

I aspire to state the theory absolutely

simply and clearly. I address it to a wide

and clever audience.

I'm ready to answer all questions

in Russian. With deep respect.

3

For the first time in a critical study, a
pioneer study, social Darwinism.
The book's main themes are immortality,
death consciousness, individual and
species, time ruins, the machine of
the world, and the imaginary
architecture of the cosmos.

4

The themes have aroused intense
interest wherever I read.
Although my work is impeccable
what is written will give rise to
overwhelming debate. Much has been said
about anger and the bible
that bears repeating. There are many bad signs.
I am encouraged that there are no books about anger
in second-hand bookstores.
People hang onto those books.
You can't scare me—I teach.
I am sure to be known as
the woman who writes about anger.

Self Portrait in Five Weddings

1

Conceived in a meteor shower.
Called down from the stars
by desire, which brings everyone into the world—
the young couple fumbling with glasses,
fighting zippers, religion, and marriage
came later, like Perseids' light, mouths
open and hearts with wow— this heavenly
shakedown of souls yearning for birth.
The fast light lost makes us reach
for a hand in the darkness—we are
stubborn in our loneliness—
for a friend, or a poem, or no one, or you
lit up like an hour on the hood of a car
at the edge of a gravel pit,
the words' or hands' or mouth's
search for the flare of now, now—
all of us born of desire.

2

And lonely as flower girls are
a dream of gloves and lace and
sweeter than anyone can remember of being
an actual kid in stiff skirts and too much hairspray.
Backcombed and crinolined within an inch
of this will in me—the refusal to smile,
steadfast and glowering, the pictures ruined for
two weddings. My aunts with their dreams of
dresses and handsome men, with grandchildren
now, where the stars are brighter in winter.
My father drove us home, no
speech, no music. In the backseat
leaning against the window to watch
the night roll over — what I
wanted then was always more.

3

If the stars are about yearning—
even when my boyfriend was the last
person I should be caught dead with
in a second-hand tuxedo shirt a decade
before retro was retro and
his biker boots stomp drunk on everything but
he's singing along to *once twice three times a lady*
and I am so hungry for what I
won't call love yet, I'll take it
where the disco ball spins above the low-lit dance floor—
that's the kind of girl the gods made me
given over to the length of the song
beneath what will stand in
for stars.

4

Off Washington's coast the tanker *Nestucca*
sent her slick greetings north for the new year's
marriage of sea water and crude oil, glimmering
ink cloud, black lake within the ocean west of the island.
Nestucca of the seabirds' tarred feathers, freezing,
drowning. So if that's the girl the gods made it's no surprise
I was on Chesterman's beach in a yellow raincoat
with the town turned out for the morning-after show
this human dirge with shovels and rakes, witnesses to
the change in me that then was love.
At night, on the beach, the sky dissolved in the
tide that pulls shoreline further out
with each suck of the sand, and small rocks
wash against themselves
where the moon rises full with that
one who claimed to hear its sound,
the o of her mouth a lunar tuning fork, humming high
and hooded, sexy as death. In the moon
and cold we were held together that night and
the days that followed
by the dark angel *Nestucca*.

5

All of us are born of desire.
So if a prairie sky lifts eyes and breath,
makes possible this starry pool table
shooting Venus in the corner pocket,
in a city with two rivers, both of them
flooding, then this surge of courage,
this slouched hip silhouetted by
June light that sets this ache in
motion or the awe in me
that's already gone—did you see that?
—make us tousle over small change
I was trying to stuff into the pocket of your
loose jeans. My hand reaching hip bone
will rename summer and yearning's radiant point,
so full of what the stars
already know about our fate and
its street lights and flooding rivers.

Three Songs: Participation Mystique

Projections change the world into the replica of
one's own unknown face.
— CARL JUNG, "The Shadow"

In the hall of Holy Name Church, when lights
turn down with brownie leaders' voices lowered,
and the long extension cord is plugged in so the
papier mâché campfire glows orange red yellow at
the centre of this circle of girls on dusty linoleum
that doesn't matter once the singing starts—sitting
cross-legged in sagging leotards, I close my blue
cat-eyes under my brown beret to better hear
how *the cruel war is raging* at the utter edge of a
beauty that makes anyone part of the girl in the
song who will *tie back my hair, men's clothing I'll
put on.* What is this gorgeous and painful heat
that opens in my chest but the sacred heart of
music, after our dues are collected and promises
declared. I don't know yet if this sound of others
or my own voice reaches to *pass as your comrade,
no one will ever know* but among thirty girls

singing together *won't you let me go with you* this is how I learn about love. There are many repetitions.

Is it my own face *I long to try something I never had* —that's unknown at nineteen with a Billie Holiday record on repeat in the attic sublet from friends who are subletting from friends; is it the windows open to July and traffic as I shuffle barefoot, hips and voice rocking together as proof that *I'd give my soul just to call you my own?* Does the music cause this slow drag in my veins now that *I've heard it said that the thrill of romance can be like a heavenly dream?* Or is it a memory residual in these vintage dresses, someone else's wartime winter, summer, repeating *where can you be?* It's just that I don't know who my friends are or what to do with this ache that I should be wary of naming. *Lover Man.*

At twenty-seven I should know better except
the Cowboy Junkies have the word junkie for
a reason and I'm in this apartment vibrating
with wedding dances, and people shouting in the
Croatian Cultural Centre parking lot, its weekend
cars and big music and skytrain whining past a
kitchen overrun with cockroaches—these things
overlooked for the song like a prayer when my
dinner is done and I'm drinking alone, singing
along down nerve endings how I've given in to
this *misguided angel hanging over me*, insisting
on *crazy and he scares me*, the slow shuffle
around the *soul like a Lucifer / black and cold
like a piece of lead*, like Heathcliff, like Ruth Ellis
dancing with a stranger, like *Fool for Love*, the
movies reiterate what the song does with the
words at my throat where the nerves jolt. All
ritual involves repetition. Dresses to die for, *love
you till I'm dead*, or almost, or until you are, or
the record stops.

The Blue Dress

I wore it for years before you saw the design
it had on me and swore then
that dress started everything
I reeled around in, brazen in
the lifted skirt, forget-me-not, the way
you held the zipper at the waist and undid me,
the dress spread out beneath us with its bluesy
pattern of cornflowers tossed
at a wedding, or wildflowers thrown
into an open grave.

When I found the blue dress in a sale' basket
on the floor at Deluxe Junk for five dollars
I wasn't looking for anything. But the
wheeling circles of its pattern opened my hands
to the drape of its weight.
The blue dress was someone's idea of
a woman dancing,
a memory recited through wars.
It paid homage to underwear, flared out from
hips, a field of lupins passed at high speed,
what a fighter pilot remembers of love.

How it hung made sense of my throat
and taught what breasts can accomplish,
how it swung its skirt into summer, a
carnival with the younger self playing
at the centre. It was cut with hunger.
It was stitched with the trailing hurt
of a saxophone note stretched long and almost
breaking,
in a wood-cut pattern like an ink sketch
of champagne bubbles in the *New Yorker*
or how cartoonists diagram thought.
But it's not about thought, the colour
of delphinium crossed with
iris, a dress made from blue sky and tears,
the skirt's wide wheel turning.

Rhubarb

Splayfoot among the rhubarb and rows of onions,
my heels cracked and soles toughened. Shoeless
days. How the red stalks and leathery leaves
separate for the knife in my hand. Rough bouquet.

We used to beg my grandmother for a stalk of
rhubarb. With icing sugar. The sour sharp and
hard against such candied chalk. The rude fruit
dragging your mouth this way, the muscles of your
eyes pulled that. Terrible and sweet like pictures
of Jesus with his chest open. Blood and good you
couldn't stop, what god made for us of birdsong
and gardens, raw peas and stolen carrots we slid
from the warm ground, knocked the earth from,
and ate.

Winter is long here with heavy foods and nothing
new until the rhubarb pushes its green excess
through grey dust. No pear tree for lovers to climb,
no cherry with its sexy red. *The darling rhubarb*

of May. Practically a weed. When I was a kid
I thought of Adam and Eve covering themselves
with rhubarb leaves. Who'd ever seen a fig tree?
My sister phones long distance to say *rhubarb
crisp* but in this house it's stewed rhubarb, my
tart darling, the rhubarb of my eye, with the
spoon to her lips saying *my mother used to make
this.* Out on the hot street in the slow stroll for ice
cream, sunburned shoulders and bare legs and slow
memories of all the food we remember from our
mothers. The people at these latitudes dreaming
of a back row where they raise a glass or a beer
bottle in praise of, or neighbours on their patios
murmuring a prayer to, rhubarb, rhubarb.

Or horseradish, which grew next to the rhubarb
in the stand outside the north fence in the
alleyway across from the stampede grounds. The
adults loved horseradish. Its stink and strength.
I too would grow up and eat things I once hated.
Sometimes you had to. Horseradish blowing in the
windy heat across from the roar of the Ponoka

stampede. Both cowboys and Indians ending up sometimes in that alleyway. We knew who puked and where. The stampede outhouse doors painted with heifer and steer. I didn't know what I was.

In Gram's house no pictures of Jesus. But after lunch, after the screen had slammed in the sun (she'd fed the old man his cold meat and fried potatoes, the coffee with canned milk from contented cows and then he was gone in green workpants and cap, truck, or tractor), the dishes done, slop bucket slung outside. In the long day's slow heat, we went barefoot in flapping laceless runners out back. Past the pump and rhubarb patch, hauling a cotton blanket and iced tea to the dry stubble where she'd cut back the alfalfa and thistle, for her *beauty rest* she called it *come on*. The blanket stretched out with magazines for ladies as she undid her bathing suit to lie on her belly, her bare back browning without strap lines in the sun.

Beneath a tie-dyed floppy hat I turned the
magazine pages, reading everything, the wide-eyed
ladies in blue eye shadow and white sandals so
happy about cottage cheese. I didn't know what
I was. A city kid on a scrubby farm where the
dishwater drained into a bucket. My grandpa's
place at the table a pile of newspapers, cribbage
board and tobacco tin, his canned milk and
contented cows, his ashtray and *dirty old man* my
gram said. There was an outhouse with two holes
and no one said why. The unused hole a gaping
portal to the unspeakable, which we confronted
daily. My gram showed me a ceramic pot I was
supposed to pee in if I had to in the night, in a
room full of dolls sitting up watching. I loved her
and she scared me. Old woman lying with her bra
off. The hot day and fly buzz. I drank my iced tea
like a lady and kept my shirt on. *Fer chrissakes*
Gram said *you've got nothing to hide!* What did
she know. I'd hidden everything. I was perfectly
empty, a clear glass filled with heat, with pond
smell and frog gossip, fly buzz and lazy. My gram
snoring a little. My boredom absolute.

Asleep, I was stretched out flat in the endless heat
when she shushed me then *shit!* up on her feet
and shrieking, the deflated sacs of her bosom—
I saw them—flapping as *shoo shoo* her shoes on,
she grabbed her straps and ran out among *shoo!*
Go on! a dozen sheep turning tail and dashing
from her furious *go on*. Their heels high and
hopping *you dumb bastards!* darting in three
directions. She scared me. *Stupid goddamn sheep
ate all my bloody rhubarb*. She emphasized the rue.
The red and green stalks chawed down to stubble.
These stupid sheep were *his* bright idea—*his* fault,
her ruined plans for pie or stewed rhubarb, this
goddamned hole of a yard and nothing on the
radio. The sheep's black eyes, indifferent, their
shorn behinds turning and leaping. Beyond where
I stood in the bristles, my feet tender among
magazines scattered, missing already the rhubarb.

Salt Lick

It is a country of erosion
between the mountains and the dry
grass plain. It is a country of forgotten
oceans, ancestors of unnamed rivers.
It is a wind-worn cabin
in the space between barn and
big house.

Made small by distance, snowy field,
the boy's insistence that
he'd pull me on the sleigh
his narrow shoulders leaning into
the idea of a man, away from
my weight in quilted pants and parka
approximating pretty.

I wanted to be the sort of girl
who knows her animal parts. The day
the calf got born and abandoned,
its mother turning from the still folded
legs, the creature who was not bawling
enough about its fate.

A country none of us knew the words for
not meadow rue or sagewort or that the fields
lie close to treaty number 7. We spoke the
ranchers' vocabulary of stockyard and
Texas gate; the boys had rifles before
they could read. Cattle paths braiding out
toward the wetlands. None of us knew
our minds were rivers that were dammed before
we met them but one thing was
certain: that for love or revenge,
one day you'd have to marry.

All day in the close house the
middle boy kept saying *what's it to ya*,
which I mis-heard *what's a tooya*—
some farm-kid riddle about sex. I couldn't
get away from my ignorance.
It was water wearing down limestone.
It was freeze and thaw and heave of
What's it to ya? repeated the way boys do
until the older brother said wanna go outside? and
led me out. First time a boy asked me to do
anything but I knew to let him pull the sled

where the dead grass clattered above snow,
and so we crossed the field.

Past willow, cattle, he pulled this
girl in glasses, the I behind their zeros a
blinking cipher, the great hollow in
the chest too small for such wind
and my one accomplishment only this
weight, acted upon, this drag in
sitting pretty and both of us silent
as if pulled away from the house
with the failing calf on the kitchen floor
toward some goal, or call in the cold.

Pulling away from, or toward, there
was force in these unspoken measures
that brought us to the fence. We climbed
through the wire he held taut,
crossed the pasture to its centre where a blue
block sat— just a rock, a cube, a
salt lick, he said. What's it to ya?
A dare or a fact? I didn't know

and wanted to, so I knelt down and
laid my tongue in one of its concave grooves.

On my knees in snow and last year's
blue stem, tongue stung by the
burn in the thirst of cattle and restless
horses, it dragged saline through my veins,
pulling between family and open plain, it
drew into blood's memory this concentrated view
of the boy so small in its distance
before we both walked back, dragging the sleigh
and our shadows behind us in the dusk.

Whether I took a turn as a force, dragged the boy
and learned to lean away from his weight
as a counter to the man he expected
to stand in as, pulling calves, taking corners.
Whether the horizon pulled us back from this
daring that involves the tongue, whether
the blue brine burned the words for
this small reprieve from acted upon, the
weight of evidence was in the work of wind,

the scripted weather that would wear us into
these hoodoo runnels, trampled paths,
this past that would pull us back where
the vet couldn't help if the cow walked away
the little one dead by dinnertime
though our mothers had fed it coffee,
and waited for us, eyed us now, their cigarettes
and sighs as if our future faces stared through
these ten-year-old kids late for
supper though they didn't see my tongue
stung with the blue secrets I'd laid down.

Not enough has been said

about cornflakes—
My grandfather reaching for the box
every morning, saying *I think I'll have cornflakes.*

about milk—
My mother's talk of
the milk they had—with
solid cream that sealed the jar.
Cream you could scoop with a knife, a tablespoon,
drop it onto cornflakes. *It was good*—
the word *good* a groan like religion, a real thing
in which you could believe. The richness of cream
so thick you could cut it. I was a child then, such
accounts were new, farm-fresh
with cornflakes, a little sugar, *it was good.*
My grandparents' kitchen, the scallop-edged
bowl my grandfather always used.

about cornflakes—
My grandmother's recipe for chicken:
crushed cornflakes with salt and pepper to coat
the chicken before roasting. We hated it
but my mother said *eat it.* How her eyes
could make us choke down anything. We ate it.

Our grandmother smiling, mistaking our
heads down for hunger.

about choices—
How cornflakes was a kind of code
in the general store. My grandmother used to
say *I'll have a box of cornflakes please*, conspiratorial
inflection on the cereal name, by which she meant—
she'd lower her voice, *kotex please*.
The girl my mother was, red-faced among her
sisters, what was there to believe in
the grocer reaching behind him,
discreet, my grandfather looking
away from women's business. This mother of daughters
buying a family-size box of "cornflakes,"
which I'm thinking about now—as I pour cereal,
slice banana, the smell of the fruit and grain
(soy milk on mine), some shame in
my line. What my mother believed in and
the secret words for what we need.

Erratic

South of the Red Deer and years
west of memory, a boulder rests miles
from its original ice sheet in
a field's wild dream scoured clean
by glacier and then this human clearing,
settlers, which mean change
where aspen competes with grassland
for sunlight.

Liminal and loam rich, at Pine Lake among
leaves trembling like tickets out of there,
a girl in the excess of her body
erratic. Her heart astringent as chokecherry
she has stepped away
from the younger sister's
croon and fumble
in scrub willow and farm boys beyond
the fire. Self-conscious between
older women with rye on ice and
sunglasses, between younger teens
at lake edge and foxtails.

Below boreal and north of grassland
only the roughest terrain remains original.
The place is cultivated by loss,
woodland caribou, whooping crane,
rivers channelled between
pussy willow and aster, kids
in bathing suits, grasses' dominion,
aspen where water collects in
what locals call scrub brush, useless
therefore natural.

She's told her body's rough terrain,
her subtle depressions and
mind competing with absence
for sunlight is natural.
She knows nothing of nature.
Her mind is a coulee full of
rough scrub, between trees and lake,
useless as this ache and yearn
or pining.

South of the rivers flowing east,
the girl heavy with wanting
she can't say what she hasn't tasted.
But a visitor has come
in the lake breeze soft as
bluebell, an avocado in an
open hand, alien as a glacial
boulder in a field where
the girl can't say if it's fruit or vegetable.
But a slice of it is in her mouth
when she hears someone cry that
Elvis Presley has died.

It is in her mouth this strange first taste
of avocado and loss, the women's talk of
when there was nothing but farmland and wild rose
between coyote and church until the king's music,
those hips and what could not be televised.

The spillways of their voices
with the radio and magpies,
bare feet beneath lawn chairs.
The girl still years from the distance she'll carry
the king of her mother's remembered youth,
the avocado's tender bitterness
for the words long held in her mouth,
not believing yet in
lonely street, so far from
the aspens, trembling.

Salt Physic

We were naked the night we went into the sea.
Our mouths briney from rock salt and olives, the
red wine's urge toward more. Not skinny dip or
moonlight whim. It was magnetic drag, I tell you,
pelagic compulsion. Even in West Vancouver, even
near lawns and living rooms. It was the full suck
of a night ocean that hauled ass—mine—into the
temperate and fertile slosh.

Hauling ass. Is that any way to say moonshine?

Redneck vocabulary, is that any way to say
sea change? Neck back belly bum. Suspended.
The disbelief, the pungent swell, the body's
displacement. And human will, is that any way to
float? My grandmother tried to teach me this but
in Crimson Lake I was too afraid. My body rigid
trying to please her, pleasing her, laughing as she
said *lie back you've got to relax*, that crazy inhaled
shriek of her laugh *Relax!* I couldn't. Could not

trust my body to hers, to anyone's. Her leading me
deeper than I'd been, afraid of the water, afraid
to put my head in. She insisted that floating is
easy—insisted I lie back in the water with my
head in her hand, the other hand holding my lower
back, my body rigid. Her rounded little bowl of
a belly she always complained about, souvenir of
pregnancies, her silly bathing cap's rubber fringes.
She said *seniors' swim class*, she said *breast
stroke lovey*, then let me go while she laid back to
demonstrate how lovely it was. Kicked her slim
feet. To lie ear-deep in a cool summer lake, to
suspend oneself, the sky overhead. Lovely, she said.

I was tentative for so long. Not trusting a hundred
things including the body. This one. Filled with
wine and swimming out to the pulse of *I'm here,
I'm here.*

To float on your back you have to get ear-deep and
let the water rise as it will. Have to let go and give
in to let the water hold you. Twenty years from
Crimson Lake, I kick my slim feet, my body at
last lying back, cool and weightless in Vancouver,
far from Alberta's tent trailers and impossible
fathers.

How did the fathers get in here, their
impossibilities? Some days still insisting on a
story's intention. Or tidy and clever formula:
blood's ionic coincidence; an ocean composition;
some salt pattern in the blood piss tears. Some
correspondence between the body's inner seas and
the conditions that make cell life possible. The
sea inside the body. The water in equal proportion
displaced by memory. In equal proportion. But
the tide pulls in what it will. Having forgotten
the periodic table of the elements, its weights and
measures, its basic molecular faith.

A story was conceived. In Red Deer. August secret
in someone else's apartment. Or in a car. Or was
there a blanket spread out beneath a pine tree,
a motive to the small fish of my father's seed, a
thirst to my mother's freshwater stream that
made this wine-soaked body rocking big now and
buoyant with friends. It suspends the disbelief.
Ear deep. Happy as a clam.

Who wouldn't think of home? Such persuasive
archetypes and returns to the sea. The Greeks
can say *fish-cold* or *wine-dark*, their ancient and
classical hearts *like a high surf running*. But when
you're from Edmonton you can't be too careful. In
Lacombe, in Rimbey, you don't say *salt* with *sex* or
sea-swelled mothers.

I had meant to keep the mothers out of this.
Had meant to keep the word *Edmonton* from a
poem. That jetsam! The psychic surge, the noise

45

in counted stations of the cross in chronological
order, where and how I lived, who my parents
really were. And then what happened? The messy
surface, the talk-show confession, the twelve-step
snake-oil recovery guarantee. Sometimes wine
is good, including excess. In deep, sounding the
depth. Where I come from, depth is suspect.
What depth? The sea has heard enough excuses.
I was surprised by floating. It was thinking of my
mother, up to my eyes in it.

I had meant to keep the mothers in this. And
weeds. Some trace of the kelpy underwater forest.
The fish and flesh. So much tempting flotsam.
When I was a girl there were sandy ruts for a road,
with grass down the centre, a track for thongs to
flap, willow trees, a bit of a hill, a rickety beach
store, a red popsicle. When I was a girl there were
violent fathers but there's no news in that. When
I was a girl there was no ocean yet, no tidal pull,
no cedars there. But I'm turning to salt from

looking back. Above the wet salt realm, the deep
untold beneath my blissful and oblivious backside.

The moon's reflection where the story about
Alberta is behind us, or beneath the surface of
the body's memory. Do I really have to say oil
boom? I am a girl in the night sea, not seen. What
the mind and muscles know by letting go, breast
stroke lovey.

That Catholic Country

of childhood, our emblem dear
Apollo landing, communion of
maple leaf plus amen
nuns with guitars, modern therefore
wonderful, all in English now, a girl in that
young city, church bells' centennial song,
everything new and me too in
the mystery and knee socks,
day of days, we sang *glory laud and*
honour, a line of girls
white-dressed and inching forward
mouths full of amen after
a year, almost, of instruction—
crayon drawings of the last
supper including haloes around everyone
the bread, the wine, the poor-me-dog-eyes
of the Lord, a word balloon over His head
that said *do this in memory of me.*
So I came home and practised
on the younger kids. On their knees,
they said amen to anything I
fed them: host in bits of Ritz crackers,
honeycomb cereal, lording it over them,
dog-eyed and pious

waiting for my Change
shot through with sacrifice and
the transubstantial possibility that even over the din of
traffic circle and pancake house the hosannah of my
heart would sing
louder than my father's Johnny Cash—
my still-unspoken hunger
my white purse stuffed with kleenex
cotton gloves folded to
the mystery of bread, of god as man
as lamb, my turn at long last
demure now I made myself
ready to fall
into a burning ring of bright flames,
the flashy miracle, divine fireball,
jesus jawbreaker, something
vigorous and surprising
but it was only a paper-thin
bland wafer dissolved before I could
say amen and shuffle back to parents who were
mouthing the words *to thee redeemer king.*

On Hiding

The thing back of the thing was the thing that
mattered.

—H.D., *HER*(*mione*)

The habit starts young in a basement closet
beneath winter coats, breathing in darkness,
leaning into the corner with
rifles wrapped in blankets, you
hold your knees to your chin, and wait. For
the boy with a wolf-skin rug on his head, your
siblings in love with him, or a mother
to come looking but no one does and
the wool coats keep
the secret that is you. Lying
in the yard beyond the house the buried
bones of horses above the rock of fossilized
things that thrived here once though no
one thinks of them or knows their names,
someone may be murmuring yours upstairs
and you'll miss lunch or the light or need
to stretch, so you open the door and give it up.

Getting lost was easier at first—the snow in
July, driving horizontal,
the wet maps, no north and
men in the bar later saying
you girls didn't cross that glacier alone?

Hiding can take place in the open. It serves
the killdeer crying here here look over here
her big noise and wing-drag a faked injury like
the idea of duller females in any species.

With practice you can hide anywhere. Dancing
in your tailored coat conceals
the ruse, smile revealing nothing
though restless now you're good at it,
still no one comes looking despite
the base tone of distant voices wondering
whatever happened to...
and you will miss friends or
need to stretch and look for
the door you can't find
because you're lost now
in a habit of camouflage,
over here, its desperate little theatre.

You've been lost before. The map's
contour lines in all the wrong directions,
storm-obscured hours committed
to error. You can cry all you like.
It's cold and no one's looking.
Choose your path or follow a channel
of the mind's branching rivers, shoulder the pack,
and start walking.

Cleavage: An Education

I was taught that men have needs which
sounded like knees when repeated but
are much more dangerous when they get going,
unstoppable and your fault like
breasts so heavy they hurt your back—there was
Auntie D who used to cry when men stared—
or so small men wouldn't look at you
and if men don't look you will go nowhere fast.

All women knew this, I mean *ladies*,
like the one at 3 AM who pounded on our door
and cried *he's going to kill me*
even after she was inside, where
my mother made coffee and said
Don't be silly and my father said
For Christ's sake when the husband hit
the door.

On the freeway there were ladies in bikinis with
big pink balloons, hand-lettered signs held just
below their bellies that read Peter Lougheed Yes Indeed!
which they pointed to, nearly naked in their
smiles, waving as cars honked at them, the way my
father did, leaning on the horn, his window

rolled down, they were asking for it,
his slap on the side of the car and his
yelping the way cowboys did on TV.

TV which meant the Dean Martin show with Gold
Diggers and Goldie Hawn insisting she wasn't
acting dumb, she was dumb like on Laugh In—
so much sex and big eyelashes, men reaching for
and women pretending not to notice.

Don't women have needs? (I would have said ladies. There
were no women yet.) Well yes, but they're different
like furniture and nice houses. I never saw one
who was happy and some were suicidal.
No one could say why.

In the neighbour's basement we
took her sister's bras, stuffed wool
work socks into 38Ds over t-shirts
bulging toward this threshold where we were
at a drive-in Kath said. *I'm the guy.* Each in her
full bra knowing/not knowing how Kath would
yawn and stretch her arms until—
no scene is stock the first time. I played my

part perfectly, my eyes on
my own bad faith out a foot in front—
the attention it took to not notice, the
guy's fingertips reaching for,
the knowledge to insist on watching the television
movie of my own soft face against his large
and wool-filled chest. Of course it was lovely and
eventually we lay down, Kath with her guy's hands
squeezing my work-sock cups
which filled and spilled with the hot ache I
understood now that my stuffed cups were crushed—
how it happened, the inevitable
veritable breath taken by Kath kissing her own hand
clasped hard over my mouth so s/he wasn't
kissing me which explained more than
the heat in my gasp, the current running through
my knees, hips, and socks.

Negatives

What remains is this half-
unreadable archive of
negatives for the mind's
dresses and corrected
thinking on dinners and beaches,
the various cats, the couple
posed, rehearsing promises,
those years before digital, their
colour values and arguments reversed,
a windup bird in
a cage, a pointing finger, yours
like your father's habit of
speech, recorded here
where every smile will
one day reverse. This is history
as shot, as caught,
except for
what the space around it
holds, waiting.

Blood Line

We think back through our mothers if we are
women.

—VIRGINIA WOOLF, A Room of One's Own

Who left the farm to finish school, who lived with
the doctor's family in town who needed a girl for
the help. Who ironed sheets, iron heated on a
wood stove—too afraid of the gas iron oh I thought
it would explode. Carrying the water, heating it
for laundry, a girl is necessary. Who later became
whose mother. Still a girl when the doctor's wife
called Rosella to help, the ohhhh arising from the
blood-soaked bed. And Rosella, in service, for her
education, who rolled up sheets that would take
days to wash, who carried the flannel-wrapped
bundle, laid it in the furnace while the doctor slept,
who fed the flames with whose secret loss.

Whose curled hair and hot pants and cork
platform shoes for the party. Who leaned over the
turkey with an electric knife, shouting instructions
for the mix and chips, whose damn bird was

falling apart, damn oh damn her hand cut through
the thumb. Whose blood was everywhere but on
the bird.

The meat of the bird overdone of course, body of
the girl undeveloped.

Who was cut and stitched, who came to school
with the daughter for *It's Wonderful Being a Girl*.
Who watched the film's maps of fallopian hoses,
its red arrows for eggs and uterine flow. Who
rolled her eyes at the mothers in the movie with
cinch-waisted dresses and flowers to arrange for
daughters who take baths in the middle of the
days marked up by free calendars and hygiene
tips for daily daintiness—everything needing
constant surveillance and scrubbing. Even the
feet were suspect. Who watched the girl in the
movie saying you don't really know what it's like
until it happens to you, who means bleeding but
can't say so, who gets a yellow dress with lace
and laughs alone in her own room. Who may have
said bullshit while walking home, liking the rough

truth of the word. Whose stitched hand held mine,
who said sometimes it feels like hell.

Whose blood serves for descent and the bond
between bleeding and serving, and this suture,
this rough truth of meat and flowers, the edges
of virtue in situ cinched with collusion, colliding
generations of a wound around what we are never
told or cannot say.

Through the Word West

Who's turned us around like this
so that whatever we do, we always have
the look of someone going away?
— RAINER MARIA RILKE,
from the Eighth *Duino Elegy*

if the mystery doesn't want to be known
it sees you from the secret ground
—BRENDA HILLMAN, "Deep Noticing"

West of the city and yearning for sleep
in fields that have not forgotten the woods
I am singing this dream that
a woman shifts gears,
her hands opening. The words
to these fields, the secret ground,
the dispersed seeds
have taken root in sorrow.

Through the word west a door
someone young is.

In rosy everlasting, her t-shirt tossed,
someone young in sweet clover
stretched out with friends in grass as tall as July.
A phrase hovering like thought, freckled girl,
someday, why not, her hips like this and hair down to
oh yeah.

The west is a sliding barrier opening and closing.
Girls talking, bergamot and sun-breasted foothills
waiting for passage, rites of a story told in dreams.
Prairie sage and larkspur, hound's tongue, paintbrush
wanting elsewhere.

In one west the first girl was given seeds,
was given loam and harvest,
her mother's view
of horizons, mystery, and a name
that means only young one, female, Kore,
that one, lit or shadowed by the mood
of her mother's circling seasons.

In my west I was given
my mother's version, turned around
like the word no.

Inside small rooms' smoke and dust,
dishes, folded towels, excuses. Origins
of the ache in my chest, someone sad was always
singing.

What you are given young one,
female one,
whether by wind or by world,
whatever you start with,
everything
wears away.

I thought I was nothing to
the famous yellow fields,
the men who wore caps that read
Rape[seed] is Beautiful.

Some said I was "all unwilling,"
but I wanted to go further than
the idea of a door.

In one version I resisted.
Some stories demand a fight, a woman saying no
to the press of switchblade against the sexual pulse
of her warm you-know-where.

In one version I was asking for it. Having lived
all my life in that impossible prefix
Unseen, untouched, until:
here is the feared thing.

This thanatos textbook
someone young always opening.

Further west the field opened into the secret places of earth.
A youth not unwilling but entranced by the perfume
　　　　　of lilies, narcissus,

though in the land of my birth the air
was filled with sage and purple clover.

There's no border there, no story but many names.
Hades. Limbo. Bardo.
Confused wandering in timeless dark.

I was admitted underground, acquired
its vocabulary of entrance, thresholds, island of stars
and horses, dark history, the abducted and missing,
mourned and countless.

Everyone knows about that gateway
except for the young. I was one of them.
Everyone knows you lose your voice, become spoken
by shadow, long nights, dramatic lighting.
In one version I was afraid
which I mistook for excitement—
something happening at last.

People who know better turn their faces from the one
whose name is dread. Now I know better too.
But then I turned my back to the sun
pulled by the charismatic lure of
being wanted, chosen, unwary as
a bouquet of narcissus in the
hand of who enthralled me.

Whether he wears a hood or resembles
a woman or no one,
whether the room's smoke screens an abyss
and I'm attracted to a precipice,
whether we're to meet at 3:00 AM at the wood's edge
when the drumming has stopped,
the many-named one has a long reach
and loved my fine ankles,
whether I was attracted to doors opening—
whose hand was on my heart?
That barrier opening and closing
a floodgate on a dammed river.

Shy as a mate, I was also queen of everything
beneath the secret places on earth.
The five rivers beginning with sorrow,
Acheron some call it, past Hope, the Fraser
and Coquihalla, Cocytus and Lethe,
Pitt River's tributaries trickle through
fields of asphodel, the dog at the gate
(there was a dog, there was a gate
though the fields were shadow gardens planted with ghost willow,
remembered lavender, and blood root, etiolated fakery
to assuage the newcomers).

It was a drag how every story
ended in death—but I was young then
mistaking gravity for depth, and didn't
suspect its pull would draw
my heart, plagiarize my face.
I'd been given ploughed fields,
gas wells, feed lots,
an industry that
profits from the underground.
The place has many names.

Say I was given a pomegranate.
Say someone young always is.

Who turned me around like this?
Who gave me this look of leaving?
Pluto, Hades, Little John, Dirk,
Dis, beggarman, Blue(beard), thief,
the name a danger for distance to speak.
Hours and years go by.

Whatever you're given, everything wears away.
The name my mother called me like a murmur
through drought and grass. Did she lie down
on the earth which was now my sky,
with a promise of rain in the reversed world?
I knew that name once
and the night.

There is a door into the story of such a union.
Someone older might open it.

It's not that I missed my mother,
but the scent of the real earth in springtime,
the dreamed garlands in a hero's welcome home.

With his raised brow and his fast horses,
my mate with his famous welcome for all
who arrive there! His rage when
a guest tries to leave.

I remember sorrow like a river
at the bottom of a canola field,
night's condensation that soaks
your hem, your loose trousers and
sandals, it clings like morning dew
when you have the look of
someone going away.

My mother came looking for me
among the wild flax and cinquefoil
but not in this version, where
I read in the dark of

coneflower and blazing star
waiting for her.
West of where the world ends.
There is no hero's welcome.

Brief Biography of One

The soul had no words for spring trees or
Calgary backyards, no country of family,
just acquired language from radio
yeah yeah yeah then swung
on a backyard swingset
in Winnipeg after a flood,
walking tiptoe to find parents
eating hot fudge sundaes,
soul's crooked bangs and religious dilemmas,
its tongue stuck on an Edmonton winter's
hoar-frosted fence.
Uprooted and moved,
the soul did not apply itself—
it interrupted others and learned
to read early except for those
mysterious three-letter acronyms
FLQ, LSD, FBI, and that one small word
it failed to read
on a Grade One blackboard: Yes.
It was kicked in the ass,
called terrible names.
It ate beet greens with butter,
knew where kittens hid in the hay.
It stood knee deep in the creek as

the snake swam past,
saw women screaming for Trudeau.
The soul got a library card,
a sketchy education.
It was bathed and shaved,
it ached and bled.
The soul ran barefoot outside with the
other girls in their babydolls,
to fit in made prank phone calls
about Robin Hood in a ten-pound bag,
knowing it wasn't original.
The soul drove on the wrong side of the road
in a vw van, its grandmother saying
I've had a long life, I get so tired of
staying in my lane.
The soul hitchhiked from Calgary,
listened to John Coltrane,
danced with k.d. lang but didn't know it.
The soul left town, books, dishes, and
carried clothes across country.
The soul discarded things, acquired things.
The soul sat with old women
dying of regret—the soul got heavy,
took photographs, lonely in the idea of years.

The soul made a move and
was terribly accused,
had wine tossed at its head,
called the cops, stayed awake all night
with a barking dog on such a short chain.
No one attends to the yelp of the soul
gulping air between barks and cries,
the outraged soul, its tall ears and disbelief.
The soul broke its chain,
left again, oh what can it carry?
but a dozen books
on a bicycle, the poets' names
like prayer beads, a bottle of scotch.
Leaving the notebooks for later,
the soul started all over again.
High River, Cochrane, the old highway,
the soul familiar with this road
and running, returning to first
places, hungry for how its lungs
fill up with setting out,
driver's seat, passing everyone,
embodied and restless.
The soul alert for change as if its life
depended upon highways.

"On December 23, 1988, the tug *Ocean Services* rammed
and holed its tow (the tanker barge *Nestucca*), off Gray's
Harbour, Washington, as the result of an improperly
maintained towline. Approximately 875 tonnes of
Bunker C crude oil was estimated to have escaped...
Numerous beaches and shoreline ecosystems along the
coast of Vancouver Island suffered oil damage. As many
as fifty-six thousand seabirds were destroyed. Bald
eagles and other raptors which fed upon oiled carcasses
were injured; herring spawning areas and crab/
shellfish populations were oiled; and traditional native
seafood was impacted." (Statistics. Summary of Spill
Events. *Environment Canada's Role in Environmental
Emergencies, 1984-1995.* www.ec.gc.ca/ee-ue. Accessed 26
February 2008.)

"Projections change the world into the replica of
one's own unknown face." (Carl Jung, "The Shadow."
Collected Works, 9ii, par. 17. Quoted in *Jung Lexicon:
A Primer of Terms and Concepts* by Daryl Sharp.
www.psychceu.com/Jung/sharplexicon.html Accessed
March 2008.)

Dance with a Stranger is a 1985 film about Ruth Ellis
who murdered her abusive boyfriend and was the last
woman to receive the death penalty in the UK. *Fool
for Love* refers to the play by Sam Shepard, which was
made into a film directed by Robert Altman (1985).

H.D. *HER(mione)*. New York: New Directions, 1981, p. 198.

74

"Its only protection is a desperate little theatre" is how
Phil Hall describes the killdeer, quoted in "Phil Hall's

Surrural: Ontario Gothic, the Killdeer, the Music of
Failure, and the Distraction of Shifting Ground" by rob
mclennan. *Poetics.ca*, no. 8, Fall 2007. www.poetics.ca

Virginia Woolf. *A Room of One's Own.*

Rainer Maria Rilke. *Duino Elegies and The Sonnets to
Orpheus.* Translated by A. Poulin Jr. Boston: Houghton
Mifflin, 1977.

Brenda Hillman, "Deep Noticing." *Loose Sugar.*
Hanover, NH: University Press of New England
(Wesleyan Poetry Series), 1997.

ACKNOWLEDGEMENTS

Earlier versions of some of these poems have previously appeared in *Hart House Review*, *Open Letter*, *Prairie Fire* and *West Coast Line*.

I am grateful to the Canada Council for the Arts for support in the early days.

This book took a long time to come into the world. I am grateful to Beth Follett for her unwavering faith and editorial acumen; to Zab Hobart for her audacious design; and to the women who run with dogs—Andrea Kwan, Miranda Ogilvie, Jane Price and Georgina Watts—who were there in literally all weather.

At different stages, the writing also benefitted from the feedback and support of many readers. "Through the Word West" was begun at Sage Hill Writing Experience in Saskatchewan. I am grateful to Nicole Brossard for her insight into pronouns. Don McKay was generous as writer in residence at Massey College. Some of the poems took inspiration from a workshop in Chicago with Lynda Barry. Other readers include: Jodey Castricano, Susan Andrews Grace, Catherine Graham, Kristjana Gunnars, Cheryl Haynes, Ralph Kolewe, Angela Larson, Jeannette Lynes, Lorie Rotenberg, D.M. Thomas and Rachel Zolf. My family in Alberta is very much a part of this work.

I am especially indebted to Suzette Mayr who was a bright light in dark times and whose tenacity and sharp wit sustained me from the earliest days. Thanks to Roy Miki for his friendship and Slavia Miki for her role as fairy godmother. This book might never have been written if Andrea Kwan hadn't opened the door with a grin. She also sent me out of town to write and otherwise made space for the book's possibility. Thank you.

ANDREA KWAN

ABOUT THE AUTHOR

Jacqueline Larson was born in and formed by Alberta.
Her work has been published in a number of journals
and shortlisted for the National Magazine award and
Hart House Review poetry prize. She makes her home
in Toronto.